GW01079970

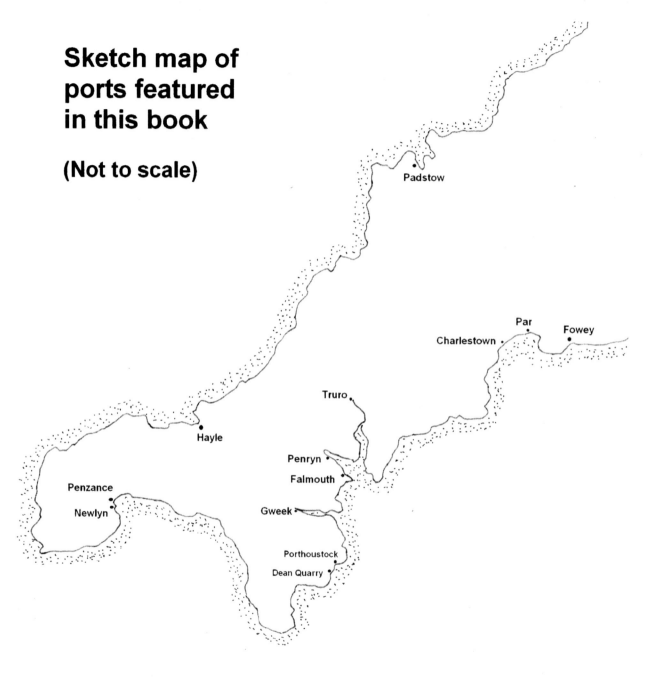

Sketch map of
ports featured
in this book

(Not to scale)

Padstow

Par
Charlestown
Fowey

Truro

Hayle

Penryn
Falmouth

Penzance
Newlyn

Gweek

Porthoustock
Dean Quarry

COASTERS OF
CORNWALL

by

Bernard McCall

INTRODUCTION

This book is a natural follow-up to *Coasters of South Devon* which was published in 2007. Trade through Cornish ports has traditionally been dominated by exports of raw materials, notably tin, stone and china clay. The ports themselves differ markedly in character from those in South Devon for they are often set in picturesque locations which offer an attractive and colourful background for the ships. Tin production is Cornwall's oldest recorded industry and exports can be traced back to the Roman settlement of the area. For many centuries, local timber was the fuel used to smelt the tin but coal had to be imported during the 18th century when the industry was expanding rapidly. Also coal was needed to fuel the steam engines used to dewater the ever-deeper mines. In the 20th century, Cornwall has become best known for the production of china clay although this industry is of comparatively recent origin, dating from the last quarter of the 18th century. Most of the clay pits were near St Austell so the ports used for export were within a small area near this town.

When English China Clays was taken over by the French-controlled multinational company Imerys in 1999, there was always a fear that globalisation would have an impact on the Cornish clay industry. That is exactly what has happened. Since 2007, it is only filler clays that have been produced in Cornwall. Imerys claims that it is cheaper to source other grades of clay elsewhere in the world, notably Brazil, and ship it to markets in northern Europe. As a consequence, the port of Par closed in mid-December 2007 and will possibly not see any further use by commercial ships. With the port of Charlestown having seen the final commercial departure in December 1999, this has left Fowey as the sole china clay exporting port in Cornwall, and here there will be a considerable reduction in exports.

Globalisation has also affected other trades. In 2005, the multinational aggregates company Cemex ceased exports from Dean Quarry.

This book looks at the ports in Cornwall that have seen commercial activity during the four decades from 1967 onwards. In *Coasters of South Devon*, we followed a route westwards and this volume continues the journey, beginning at Fowey and finishing at Padstow on the north coast of Cornwall.

I am indebted to many individuals and organisations who have given assistance, sometimes unwittingly, during the compilation of this book. Thanks must firstly go to the photographers who have made their work available for inclusion in the book. Each photograph is credited accordingly. In researching the histories of the ships, I acknowledge the help given by *Lloyd's Register* and *Marine News* (the monthly journal of the World Ship Society) and various publications from the Ships in Focus series. I am always reluctant to name individuals because I fear that others whom I fail to mention may be offended by any such unintentional omission. I must, however, give special thanks to Dag Bakka Jr, Bert Kruidhof and Bent Mikkelsen who have always been ready to answer questions about ships in their respective countries. Also much help has been given by Stuart Williams, of South Coast UK, along with William A Holmes and Tony & Krispen Atkinson who all have extensive knowledge of the shipping scene in Cornwall. As always, Gil Mayes has read through drafts of the book and suggested corrections and improvements. Any faults that remain are my own responsibility.

Bernard McCall   Portishead   June 2008

Copyright © 2008 by Bernard McCall. The right of Bernard McCall to be identified as author of this work has been asserted by him in accordance with the Copyright, Design and Patent Act 1998.

All rights reserved. No part of this publication may be reproduced, stored in a retrieval system or transmitted in any form or by any means (electronic, digital, mechanical, photocopying, recording or otherwise) without prior permission of the publisher.

Published by Bernard McCall, 400 Nore Road, Portishead, Bristol, BS20 8EZ, England. Website : www.coastalshipping.co.uk
Telephone/fax : 01275 846178. E-mail : bernard@coastalshipping.co.uk
All distribution enquiries should be addressed to the publisher.

Printed by Amadeus Press, Ezra House, West 26 Business Park, Cleckheaton, West Yorkshire, BD19 4TQ
Telephone : 01274 863210; fax : 01274 863211; e-mail : info@amadeuspress.co.uk; website : www.amadeuspress.co.uk

ISBN : 978-1-902953-35-9

Front cover : Coasters in the Nielsen & Bresling fleet were regular callers at ports in Devon and Cornwall throughout the 1960s and 1970s. They would often bring timber from Swedish ports and then load china clay for the return voyage to Scandinavia. Seen at Fowey on 15 April 1967, the **Astrid Bres** (DNK, 399grt/62) was built at the J J Sietas shipyard in Hamburg and was launched on 1 April 1962 with delivery to her owners being made on 5 May. After a decade in the fleet, she was sold on and passed through the hands of various Danish owners until 1996. During this time, she was renamed **Kim** (1972), **Ida Baagø** (1984) and **Tina Star** (1988). Sold to owners in Tortola in December 1996, it was not until 10 November 1997 that she left Søby for the Caribbean. In 2000 she was sold and renamed **Tobago Star** and five years later she was noted in very poor condition at Chaguaramas, Trinidad. In this view, she is passing the **Cimbria** (DNK, 3499grt/63) berthed at No. 3 jetty.

(the late Peter Townsend, Ron Baker collection)

Back cover : A panoramic view of Charlestown as the **Eben Haezer** (NLD, 439grt/64) arrives on 31 August 1986. Further details of the coaster are on page 26.

(Cedric Catt)

We begin at Fowey, the town taking its name from the river on which it stands. Long dominated by exports of china clay, the deepwater of the harbour has allowed vessels up to 10,000 tonnes deadweight to load at its quaysides. There are many vantage points for photography and the ready availability of self-drive motor boats to sail through the port's sheltered waters has made it very popular with ship photographers. This fine view, taken on 10 June 1967, shows part of the port area as it was before the start of the modernisation plan discussed in more detail on page 7. Clearly visible in the rail sidings on the quayside are the distinctive rail wagons, known as "hoods". There has always been a flourishing export trade shipping china clay to Scandinavia, especially Finland, where much of it is used in the paper industry. Russian ships have always featured prominently in this trade and the *Ukraina* (RUS, 2683grt/57), loading at No. 3 jetty, exemplifies a class of vessel which typified the Russian merchant fleet in the 1950s. Built at the A Warskiego shipyard in Szczecin and launched on 27 April 1957, she was one of 41 ships in the series that was known as Type B32. As far as is known, she was eventually scrapped in Russia in 1979.

(the late Peter Townsend, Ron Baker collection)

Although active in the 14th century, the harbour at Fowey did not really flourish until the latter half of the 19th century. In 1869, china clay exports began after a railway line was opened linking Fowey to Lostwithiel and a new pier built at Carne Point. The deep water in the harbour meant that large ships could access this pier and be loaded at any state of the tide. With older china clay ports unable to cope with the demand, new jetties were built upriver of the old town. This photograph was taken on 15 April 1967 and we see the **Marina** (DEU, 1000grt/66) at No. 4 jetty. The presence of two rail tank wagons suggests that she was taking bunkers at the time of the photograph. During the modernisation that would take place over the next five years, the rail connection between Par and Fowey was converted to a private road giving direct access to No. 3 and No. 4 jetty. The ship was less than one year old, having been launched at the Elsflether Werft shipyard on 20 August 1966 and delivered to her Bremen-based owner one month later. She had only one change of identity in her career, being renamed **Maria Pia M** following sale to Italian owners in 1973. She had a career of twenty years, capsizing off Cape Colonne on 11 March 1986 when on passage from Chioggia to Tripoli.

(the late Peter Townsend, Ron Baker collection)

To complete this group of three photographs showing the changes of the late 1960s and early 1970s, we find construction of the vast new storage shed underway on 25 August 1973. The **Makiri Smits** (NLD, 1600grt/73) was delivered to Marinus Smits and remained in this owner's fleet until sold to Cypriot flag interests in September 1984, her name being abbreviated to **Makiri**. A further abbreviation to **Kiri** came in 1992 following sale in mid-December 1991. In May 1994 she was sold to Norwegian owners and in September was renamed **Frakt**, this soon being amended to **Tri Frakt**. Working in the bulk trades mainly in Norway and Denmark, she was rebuilt in 1994 as a self-discharging ship and fitted with a Volvo EC-450 excavator by her Norwegian owners although *Lloyd's Register* continues to list her as equipped with the single 8-tonne crane which she had when built.

(the late Peter Townsend, Ron Baker collection)

With No. 5 jetty used only very occasionally for loading bagged cargoes of clay and even more rarely for handling other commodities, we now move on to No. 6 jetty and firstly see the **Sybille** (DEU, 999grt/77) loading on 13 June 1980. One of only three Japanese-built vessels in this book, she was a product of the Watanabe Zosen shipyard in Hakata. There were 17 coasters in the "Fastbox" series all built between 1976 and 1977 in seven different small shipyards in Japan. Launched on 7 August 1976 and delivered on 19 July 1977, the **Sybille** was the last of four from the Watanabe yard. In 1988, she was renamed **Scot Venture** for the duration of a charter to Scotline and then **Echo Carrier** for a further short charter, reverting to **Sybille** in 1989. Acquired by Irish owners, she was renamed **Rockabill** in 1991 and then **Sea Boyne** in 1993. The Fastbox vessels have given good service to their owners for over three decades, the **Sybille** remaining in service as **Sea Osprey** since 1999.

(the late Peter Townsend, World Ship Photo Library)

With the huge china clay store dominating the background, it is easy to overlook the fact there were changes between the date of the above photograph and this one of the **Kazim Genc** (TUR, 2618gt/93) taken on 22 June 2005 as she was loading for Beirut. The most notable change is that the mobile loaders used for the **Sybille** have been replaced by a permanent loader linked directly to the store. The ship was built at the Tuzla shipyard of Torgem Gemi Insaat Sanayii ve Ticaret. Although launched in 1990, she was not delivered until 1993. We do not know the reason for this delay. She is equipped with three 10-tonne cranes.

(Nick Reynolds)

There was a significant development at Fowey in 1968. At that time, the docks were owned by British Railways (BR). In that year, an agreement was made between BR and English China Clays, the main producer of china clay, according to which BR would retain ownership but ECC Ports Ltd would lease and manage the port installations and take responsibility for a modernisation scheme to last three years. Also, all freight would be routed to Fowey via Lostwithiel; the sidings can be seen in this photograph along with a diesel shunting locomotive. As already noted, the railway line between Fowey and Par was closed and turned into a private road for lorries conveying clay. The modernisation programme of the late 1960s and early 1970s saw the demolition of No. 7 jetty. The farthest inland of all the commercial jetties is No. 8 and it is here that the **Heemskerkgracht** (NLD, 2145grt/82) was photographed on 8 October 1992 as she was loading for Kemi. The ship was built for the Amsterdam-based Spliethoff shipping company by Miho Zosensho KK at Shimizu. Sold to Jakarta-based owners in 2000, she was renamed **Megah Dua** and remains in service.

(Cedric Catt)

The last decade of the 20th century saw significant changes in the shipping scene in the china clay ports. The traditional coasters of the 1950s and 1960s were nearing the end of their lives and were being sold out of northern Europe. At the same time, Russian vessels were becoming more widely seen as they tried to earn currency following the collapse of the Soviet Union. They were also undercutting freight rates. At the buoys off No. 8 jetty, we see the *Kapitan Manaseyev* (RUS, 2470gt/73), awaiting her turn to load for Sundsvall on 6 May 1996 having arrived from Liverpool. At this time, the crews of many Russian ships were buying cars to take back home either for their own use or re-sale and the cars were stored on the hatch covers. Russian-made Ladas were the favoured vehicles. The ship was built at the Krasnoye Sormovo shipyard in Nizhniy Novgorod (known as Gorkiy in the Soviet era) as *Sormovskiy-30*, her name change coming in 1978. Later name changes saw her become *Muron* in 1999 and *Valeriy Godlevskiy* in 2006. Berthed at No. 8 jetty is the *Polaris* (DEU, 7944gt/88) which was loading for Kotka.

(Cedric Catt)

In addition to those off No. 8 jetty, buoys were located at several points in the harbour and during busy periods ships were be moored to these buoys whilst awaiting their turn to load and perhaps cleaning out holds ready for inspection. Holds had to be scrupulously clean in order to carry cargoes of china clay and ball clay. Photographed in August 1972 and sporting the distinctive Schulte & Bruns hull and funnel colours, the **Randzel** (DEU, 1427gt/68) was built at the company's own shipyard in Emden and was launched on 7 February 1968. After a comparatively short life, she was broken up at Elsfleth where she arrived on 20 April 1984.

(the late Peter Townsend, Ron Baker collection)

The Cairn Line, established in the late 19th century, was eventually subsumed within the huge Furness Withy company, although its name was revived in the 1960s. The **Cairnrover** (1599grt/72), photographed on 27 August 1972, was launched from the Bodewes shipyard in Martenshoek on 10 December 1971 and completed in March 1972. Sold in 1978 to Greek owners and renamed **Giannis**, the ship was destined to have a series of later names becoming **Anastassia** (1984), **Anastassia Ena** (1986), **Reida** (1986) **Star** (1993), **Vega** (1994), **B. Venture** (2000) and **Aldebaran V** (2001).

(the late Peter Townsend, Ron Baker collection)

We briefly return to No. 3 jetty to see the **Pandor** (DEU, 499grt/80) and **Widor** (DEU, 499grt/87) wait to load china clay slurry on 4 April 1988. The **Pandor** would load for Lanaken, near Maastricht on the River Maas, whilst the **Widor** would take her cargo to St Etienne du Rouvray on the River Seine upriver from Rouen. To handle these cargoes of slurry, six ships were built, five of them at the J J Sietas shipyard on the outskirts of Hamburg. Two of the other four ships will be seen on page 19. The ships were fitted with tanks fore and aft in the holds for the carriage of slurry and they were able to carry steel or bulk cargoes on the return voyage. Although both the **Pandor**, launched on 5 March 1980, and **Widor**, launched on 24 November 1987, are of the Type 104b design from the Sietas yard, readers will be able to see some detail differences between them. The **Pandor** was sold and renamed **Wiebke D** in 1997 but it was not until 2004 that the **Widor** was sold, becoming **Laguepe** and entering service between Mediterranean ports and the River Rhône.

(Cedric Catt)

There are many vantage points to observe the ships at Fowey. In the mornings, the photographer is advised to be on the Polruan side of the river whilst in the afternoon and evening, Fowey itself offers the best opportunities. A popular location is Caffa Mill where there is a convenient riverside car park and refreshments are available in a cafe near the site of the former railway station. The **Vios** (NLD, 1999gt/90) is seen passing Caffa Mill fully laden on 21 April 2000. In the middle distance to the left, a coaster can just be discerned loading at No. 3 jetty. Nearer the camera is the slipway of the Bodinnick ferry along with a spare ferry. The ferry has been replaced by a newer one since this photograph was taken. The **Vios** was built at the Ferus Smit shipyard in Westerbroek and was launched as **Morgenstond II** in October 1990, being handed over to her Dutch owners on 11 November. She was renamed **Vios** following sale within the Netherlands in 1997 and left Dutch ownership when bought by Estonian owners and renamed **Sylve** in 2001.

(Bernard McCall)

11

Fowey was one of comparatively few places in north-west Europe where small vessels of classic bridge-amidships design could still be seen in the 1980s. The most frequent callers were two Spanish vessels, one of which is seen here as she passes Caffa Mill on 28 July 1981 at the start of a voyage to Genoa. The **Caleyo** (ESP, 2517grt/60) was built at the Duro-Felguera shipyard in Gijon. Launched on 1 April 1960 as **Venturo**, she became **Caleyo** within a few months of entering service. When this photograph was taken, she was almost at the end of her career under the Spanish flag for she was sold later in 1981 to Greek owners and renamed **Stefanos**. She was ultimately sold for demolition at Gadani Beach where she arrived in January 1989.

(Bernard McCall)

By a strange coincidence, having just seen a vessel originally named **Venturo**, we now see a very different type of coaster named **Ventura**. Of 1326gt, she was launched at the Bodewes Gruno shipyard in Foxhol on 21 April 1972 and delivered to Beck's Scheepvaartkantoor in July of that year. Sold within the Netherlands in 1994, she was renamed **Hendrik B** but it seemed as though she was about to meet a premature end when she suffered severe damage in heavy weather during a voyage from Uddevalla to Reykjavik on 29 December 1994. After being towed to the latter port for discharge and temporary repairs, she arrived at Delfzijl in late January 1995 and was declared a constructive total loss. Repairs were carried out, however, and she was sold to Rochester-based Thomas Watson (Shipping) Ltd by whom she was renamed **Lady Sandra**. Sold on two years later, she was renamed **Oak** and has retained that name through further sales. At the time of writing, she trades between Laayoune in Morocco, Las Palmas and Tenerife.

On the bank of the river and visible just ahead of the coaster's bridge is a rather dilapidated house. This was the house in which Daphne du Maurier once lived and where she developed such a fondness for the town of Fowey. Adjacent to the Bodinnick ferry slipway and formerly a boat house, the family named the house Ferryside. Thankfully, it has been renovated since this photograph was taken on 30 March 1989.

(Bernard McCall)

On fine days in the holiday season it is possible to hire self-drive boats from the Town Quay and from these boats any vantage point can be chosen. Here we offer just two views of vessels underway. The **Marc Trader** (ATG, 1301gt/83) was photographed on 30 July 1999. Built at the Hermann Sürken shipyard in Papenburg, she was delivered as **Marc L** in November 1983. She became **Marc Trader** in 1996 and was sold to operators in the Middle East in 2003, becoming **Ya Ali** and then in 2005 **Ya Haydar**. She now trades along the coast of Iran.

(Richard McCart)

The **Janet-C** (2748gt/98) arrives at Fowey from Lisbon on 15 April 2003 and will load a cargo of clay for Trois-Rivières on the northern bank of the St Lawrence River, midway between Quebec and Montreal and a centre of paper and pulp manufacture since the 1930s. Over the last two decades, many shipbuilders in northern Europe have come to realise the economies of subcontracting the construction of hulls to yards in central and eastern Europe where steel and labour costs have been much cheaper. The hull of this ship was built at the SevMash shipyard in the Russian port of Severodvinsk. It was towed from there to the Damen shipyard in Foxhol for fitting out.

(Dominic McCall)

Polruan is the vantage point for this view of the **Kalmarvind** (SWE, 1599grt/72) as she leaves Fowey with a full cargo on 19 July 1975. She was launched at the Båtservice shipyard in Arendal on 21 March 1972. Sold by her Swedish owners in 1979, she was renamed **Zuidwal** and then **Niaga 42** three years later. At that time she was trading in the Far East for Indonesian owners. Her final change of identity came in 1994 when she was sold within Indonesia and renamed **Rachmanuel 3**. It was under this name that she arrived at Chittagong for demolition on 24 March 2004.

(the late Peter Townsend, Ron Baker collection)

We now move to Par whose harbour opened in 1828 following the construction of a railway to the port from the china clay area a few miles inland. The port grew steadily and reached its heyday in the mid-1960s. The port was expanded at this time by the construction of two new berths and then the addition of a new mechanical drying plant along with new access roads. In September 1966, an average of 25,000 tons of clay was being exported each week and it was common to see every berth occupied with up to sixteen ships anchored in St Austell Bay awaiting their turn to load. The main quay at Par, on the eastern side of the harbour, was known as Long Arm or Long Wall. Port handbooks in the 1970s noted that it had six berths and all of these are occupied in this panoramic view taken on 3 August 1968. The number of berths had been reduced to five a decade later. When the port closed in December 2007, there were just two berths on the Long Arm. The reduction is easily explained when one considers that modern vessels are at least twice as long as those calling in the 1970s.

(the late Peter Townsend, World Ship Photo Library)

Photographed on 7 September 1986, the **Delta-G** (499grt/58) had arrived from Glasson Dock and was loading china clay for Glückstadt. She was built at the Makkum yard of C Amels & Zoon for Dutch owners and was originally named **Delta**. In December 1976, she was acquired by Jersey-based owners and in mid-February 1977 was renamed **Delta-G**. Her end came on 10 May 1987 when she sank off Varberg on the west coast of Sweden after her cargo of fertiliser had shifted during a heavy storm. At the time she was on passage from Landskrona to Barton-on-Humber. Her crew was rescued by the Swedish coastguard service. The **Harmony** (MLT, 424grt/63) was waiting to load a cargo of clay for Algeciras. She was built at the J J Sietas shipyard and was the second of the nine examples of the Type 37 design. Originally named **Imme**, she became **Trabant** in 1971, **Aroselle** in 1976 and then **Harmony** in 1984. Latterly she has been trading in the Caribbean and in November 2007 was sold to Miami-based owners who gave her the name **Jireh**.

(Cedric Catt)

A popular vantage point at Par has always been the western breakwater at the harbour entrance. This gives superb views towards St Austell Bay and into the harbour. Viewed from the breakwater and loading a bulk cargo at Par's No. 5 berth on 21 April 2000 is the *Nandia* (CYP, 1939gt/82), an example of the Type 110 design from the J J Sietas shipyard. She was launched as *Katja* on 25 October 1982 and delivered two months later. In 1990, she became *Birte Wehr* and then *Humber Star* in 1995. In mid-January 1999 she reverted to *Birte Wehr* but six months later was renamed *Nandia* and retained this name until sold to Turkish interests and renamed *Miktat N* in 2004.

(Bernard McCall)

The distinctive light green hulls of ships in the Marinus Smits fleet were often seen in Cornish ports; indeed we have already seen the **Makiri Smits** on page 5. The **Willy Smits** (NLD, 624grt/67), photographed on 17 August 1974, was built at the de Groot & van Vliet shipyard in Slikkerveer. She was launched on 21 April 1967 and was the last of a class of seven sisterships built at the yard. Owner Marinus Smits, although Dutch, was living in Denmark and the six ships built for his account were delivered for trade under the Danish flag, this ship being handed over as **Gerda Priva** on 26 May 1967. It was in 1971 that she transferred to the Dutch flag as **Willy Smits**. Initially 57,37 metres long and of 499grt, she was lengthened by her original builders to 65,49 metres in 1973. In December 1982, she was sold to owners who transferred her to the Netherlands Antilles flag as **Willy**. Later sales saw her become **Agny** in 1985, **Benhill Star** in 1988, **Matorma** in 1990 and **Defi** in 1992. She was thought to be still in service as recently as March 2006. The tall building in the background belonged to Cornwall Mills Ltd and housed crushing machinery for the production of molochite. Cargoes of felspar used to be imported to Par, usually from Kragero in Norway, and this was used in the production of molochite.

(the late Peter Townsend, Ron Baker collection)

To serve the various china clay dryers in the Par and St Austell areas, there was a need to import fuel oil which was discharged at No. 8 berth, the most westerly one in Par harbour. The **Onward Mariner** (239grt/70) is typical of the small tankers seen at Par before larger Everard vessels were used in the 1990s. She was built at Knottingley by J Harker (Shipyards) Ltd for Fleetwood Tankers Ltd. This company was established in the mid-1950s to deliver bunker fuel to trawlers working out of Fleetwood. Its tankers were also used to deliver petroleum products to ports in Scotland. The decline in the Fleetwood trawler fleet in the late 1970s saw her eventually chartered to Allantone Supplies, of Felixstowe, in 1985. She remained in their ownership or on charter to them for the next twenty years, being based either in the Thames/Medway or Plymouth areas but always retaining her Fleetwood registry. She was eventually sold in 2006 to become a houseboat and at the time of writing in early 2008 conversion was underway at Hoo on the River Medway. Here we see the **Onward Mariner** as she prepares to leave the berth with the assistance of the Par pilot boat on 8 October 1992. On the quayside can be seen the pipework and gantry used in the loading of slurry.

(Cedric Catt)

In addition to china clay loaded as bulk or bagged cargo, it was also loaded in slurry form as noted on the previous page. Two of the regular callers are seen here, along with the small tug **Penleath** usually based at Fowey and possibly standing in at Par for the usual pilot boat. Loading for Moerdijk, the **Eldor** (DEU, 1441/81), was built at the J J Sietas shipyard in Hamburg and was the second of the three examples of that yard's Type 104b standard design, the others having been seen on page 10. She was launched on 4 June 1981 and delivered in August. The **Tudor** (DEU, 1296gt/84), ex **Kirsten**-89, loading for Nijmegen, was a unique example of the Type 128 design from the Sietas yard. Both ships were fitted with four stainless steel wing tanks in holds 1 and 3 for the carriage of clay slurry and were owned by Paul Häse, of Hammah. They were sold in 2002 with the **Eldor** going to Danish owners and renamed **Amanda** while the **Tudor** was sold to RMS and was renamed **RMS Homberg**. Their tanks were removed on sale. In addition to the six ships owned by Paul Häse, the **Union-Elisabeth** (NLD, 1905gt/97) has taken cargoes of slurry.

(Cedric Catt)

On 21 September 1986, the **Sebastian** (ATG, 424grt/64) lies at what is now known as Berth 4 on the Short Arm, a berth in shadow for a large part of the day. She had arrived from Silloth and was waiting to load china clay for delivery to Bremen. She was built at the Schlichting Werft shipyard in Travemünde and delivered to her original owners as **Nordlicht II** on 24 September 1964 having been launched on 6 August. In 1975, she was renamed **Steinburg**, later becoming **Sebastian** on 9 April 1985 and **Stadt Wangen** in January 1988. This photograph was taken at the beginning of the flood tide. The western breakwater can be clearly seen in the middle distance.

(Cedric Catt)

In September 1966, an average of 25,000 tons of clay was being exported over the quaysides at Par each week and it was common to see every berth occupied with up to a dozen further ships anchored in St Austell Bay awaiting their turn to load. By the end of the 20th century, these volumes had decreased and fewer ships were seen. As noted elsewhere in this book, Russian sea/river ships were becoming frequent callers at the china clay ports and they offered a much increased deadweight capacity over the coasters of the 1960s and 1970s. The

Aleksandr Grin (RUS, 2319gt/97) was photographed at No. 3 berth as she was waiting to load for Rauma on 23 January 2000. She was to load china clay at Plymouth and Fowey later in the year. Her deadweight tonnage of 3030 compares to the 1115 of the *Sebastian* on the previous page and the 860 of the *Stiren* on page 25. The *Aleksandr Grin* was built at the Volgograd Shipbuilding Plant and was the last of five vessels designated Project 16291 in the Russian merchant fleet.

(Krispen Atkinson)

Our last two photographs at Par were taken from the western breakwater on the same day. The *Apricity* (692grt/67) heads into St Austell Bay on 4 June 1974. Launched on 11 October 1966 and delivered in June 1967, she was the second of a pair of sisterships built for F T Everard by Clelands Shipbuilding Co Ltd, Wallsend. Both ships were intended for the timber trade from Scandinavia to the River Trent. In 1974, they were fitted with new engines and, with the ships then working in the general and bulk trades, the cargo handling gear was removed two years later. In December 1982, she was sold to Carisbrooke Shipping and renamed *Heleen-C*, remaining with this company for almost six years. In 1989, following sale, she was renamed *Ernest T* and then *Ernest I* later that year. She was also fitted with a further "new" engine in late 1989, this being a reconditioned engine dating from 1967. Transferred to Iranian registry and renamed *Shad 1* in 1991, she may well still be in service.

(the late Peter Townsend, World Ship Photo Library)

Construction of the breakwater began in 1829 when J T Austen, who took the family name of Treffry after the death of his mother-in-law, sought to use Par in order to export copper from his mine and enclosed an area of some 36 acres once the breakwater had been built. We remain on the breakwater and look again at the Long Arm in its heyday. Nearest the camera is the **Stiren** (FRA, 499grt/59). The number of coasters flying the French flag has always been limited, but several examples used to visit Par in the late 1960s and 1970s. Many were former Dutch vessels, the **Stiren** having been built as **Timca** for well-known Amsterdam owner Spliethoff. Sold to French owners in 1967, she was renamed and traded as **Stiren** for a decade before being sold on to Panamanian-flag operators by whom she was renamed **Tor Bay**. On 13 December 1978, she grounded in the mouth of the River Douro off Leixoes and subsequently broke in two.

(the late Peter Townsend, Ron Baker collection)

Some would say that Charlestown is the most interesting of the china clay ports. It was originally called West Polmear but was renamed after its builder Charles Rashleigh who had interests in several local mines. The harbour, designed by John Smeaton, opened in the early 19th century and, like so many Cornish ports, initially its main export was copper. China clay exports soon began to dominate and the port prospered thanks to these and to imports of coal. The fascinating sight of a coaster arriving or departing through the tricky entrance has always attracted onlookers. On 17 August 1986, a large crowd has gathered to see the

Eben Haezer (NLD, 439grt/64) as she arrives from Rotterdam to load 700 tonnes of china clay for Kampen. An interesting vessel, she was built at the Hamburg shipyard of Norderwerft Koser & Meyer as *Elke Flint*. Launched on 8 June 1964, she must have been almost complete then for she was delivered only 21 days later. She was lengthened by 8,4 metres in 1975. Sold in December 1981, she was renamed *Pionier* and then became *Eben Haezer* on 12 December 1984. In October 1987, she was renamed *Martini* and then *Marina* in 1991.

(Cedric Catt)

Taken on 31 March 1986, this is a photograph of considerable interest. The **Brendonian** (604grt/66) was built for J Wharton (Shipping) Ltd by the Goole Shipbuilding & Repairing Co Ltd. She was launched on 21 April 1966 and completed as **Brendonia** in late May, the simple addition of the letter 'n' to her name coming in October 1984 after she had been sold to Captain Michael Whiting. He kept her for 16 years before she was sold in 2000 and was renamed **Shaskia Lee**. Later name changes saw her become **Sea Song** in 2004 and **Ocean Song** in 2005. The **Elfi** (397grt/59) was launched at the Barkmeijer shipyard in Vierverlaten on 18 December 1958 and handed over to Wm H Müller & Co (Batavier) Ltd, of London, on 2 April 1959. Of low air draught, she was designed for that company's liner service between London and Paris. In 1970 she was acquired by Metcalf Motor Coasters and renamed **Thomas M**, becoming **Joan T** after purchase by Captain Michael Tyrrell, of Arklow. Following sale to Isle of Man owners, she was renamed **Elfi** in 1986 but this name proved to be her last. Whilst on passage from Beckingham to Bremen, her cargo shifted and she capsized on 2 March 1987. Her crew of four was rescued. In this photograph she is about to discharge fertiliser from Hamburg.

(Cedric Catt)

The **Zanzibar** (CYP, 387grt/54) was photographed on 14 March 1976. She had arrived the previous day from Manchester and sailed the following day to Kampen. Four years later, this coaster replaced the **Fretherne** in the ownership of Captain Kenneth Shaw (see page 68). Both ships were in service for a while before the **Fretherne** was laid up and sold. The **Zanzibar** was built at the Volharding shipyard in Foxhol and retained the same name throughout her career although Captain Shaw used the flag of Panama to minimise costs at a time when it was becoming increasingly difficult to trade such a small coaster economically. Retiring in 1991 when 75 years of age, Captain Shaw sold the **Zanzibar** to owners in Nigeria and her end came on 13 January 1996 when she sank at the quayside when loading in Apapa/Lagos.

(Terry Nelder)

The **Margreet** (NLD, 397grt/61) is a fine example of standard design of Dutch coaster dating from the late 1950s, many of which were owned by the Wagenborg company and whose names ended in -**borg**. Others will be seen in this book. A product of the Friesland shipyard in Lemmer, this coaster was originally named **Schieborg**. She was renamed **Bonny** in 1972 and **Margreet** in 1976. By a strange coincidence, the author had paid his first visit to Charlestown on the day before this photograph was taken. The **Margreet** was then berthed on the opposite side of the harbour and bore different funnel colours. Sold in 1983, she was renamed **Mrs White**, later becoming **Ellenaki** in 1987, **Helena Sea** in 1989 and **Melinda D** in 1997. Berthed ahead of the **Margreet** is the **August von Allworden** (DEU, 429grt/58), built by J J Sietas. She has appeared as **Star Libra** in other volumes so on this occasion we merely list her names. Built as **Ernst de Buhr** and becoming **August von Allworden** in 1965, her later names were **Hohensee** (1982), **Star Libra** (1985), **Vasant** (1990), **Crystal V** (1991), **Kati K** (1995) and **Rika** (2002).

(Cedric Catt)

We do not have to wait long to see a sister vessel of the **Margreet**. The **Mary Coast** (386grt/61) was built by Scheepswerf "Appingedam" as **Vechtborg** and launched on 21 February 1961. She remained in the Wagenborg fleet until 1972 when sold and renamed **Esperance**. In the following year, she was renamed **Noordster** and then **Finlandia** in 1975. A decade later, she was acquired initially by Harris & Dixon (Shipbrokers) Ltd and then by Captain Derick Goubert, a Guernsey-based captain who had long cherished the ambition of owning his own ship even at a time when that had become very problematical. The ship was now named **Mary Coast**. Sold to a Caribbean owner in 1990, she was renamed **Compasion de l'Eternal**. Later changes of identity have seen her become **Key Biscayne** (1991), **Splash** (1993), **Key Biscayne** again (1995) and **Richell**

Valeria (1995). The **Thamwell** (399grt/63) was built at the Bodewes shipyard in Hoogezand as **Victress** for Beck's Scheepvaartkantoor, of Groningen. She came into British ownership in 1981 when operated by Thames & Orwell Agencies Ltd, from which she took her new name of **Thamwell**. Seven years later, she was sold and renamed **Maenporth**, this being the name of a village on Falmouth Bay. Becoming **Marystan** in 1990, she continued to trade to Charlestown until leaving northern Europe for the Caribbean in November 1992. Both ships are thought to be still trading in the Caribbean. This photograph was taken on 8 August 1985. The **Mary Coast** had arrived from Exmouth to load clay for Rotterdam whilst the **Thamwell** was discharging fertiliser from Hamburg.

(Cedric Catt)

When looking through the selection of photographs for possible inclusion in this book, it was surprising how few showed a ship loading clay at Charlestown. Seen on 5 October 1984, the **Elias Jr** (PAN, 397grt/61) has almost completed loading her cargo of china clay for delivery to Kampen. Her appearance makes it a hat-trick of Wagenborg standard coasters. She followed the **Margreet** from the Friesland shipyard at Lemmer and was launched as **Dintelborg** on 10 March 1961. Delivered to Wagenborg on 25 April 1961, she was sold and renamed **St Michael** in 1975, then **Mieke-W** in 1978 before becoming **Elias Jr** in 1980. Sold to Greek owners in 1986, she was then named **Melani** but reverted to her original name of **Dintelborg** in 1997 when sold to Caribbean operators. As such she was beached on Isla Margerita, Venezuela, on 20 January 2001.

(Cedric Catt)

By the late 20th century, china clay exports were declining rapidly as coasters were becoming larger and thus unable to access the port. Ownership of the port passed through various companies who saw the future in tourism rather than clay exports. We leave Charlestown with further views of an arrival and a departure. Arriving on 19 April 1985, the *Theo* (461grt/63) was built by J Pollock, Sons & Co Ltd, Faversham. She was originally named *The Duchess* and was built for J Hay & Sons Ltd, of Glasgow, a company which F T Everard had acquired in 1956. She had the distinction of being the last ship to bear a Hay name. In 1972, her original Newbury diesel engine was replaced by a Mirrlees Blackstone engine. She was sold in 1981 when she took the name *Theo*. A sale to Dutch operators in 1989 saw her renamed *Marjan*. She spent most of summer 1993 in Groningen and then Rotterdam, being renamed *Marja* at this period. It is doubtful if she traded as such. She remained at Rotterdam until disappearing from movement reports in March 1994 and she was scrapped by early the following year.

(Bernard McCall)

It is appropriate that our final view of Charlestown sees another of the standard Dutch coasters built for Wagenborg ownership or charter between 1957 and 1962. Like all ships the **Alk** (NLD, 397grt/62) leaves Charlestown stern first, having loaded for Kampen on 19 April 1985. She was the only one of the series to be built by Makkum Dok & Scheepsbouw. Launched on 2 March 1962, she was delivered to the Wagenborg company as **Noordborg**, becoming **Azolla** in 1975 and **Alk** in 1978. It seemed as though her end had come when she suffered grounding damage at Wells-next-the-Sea in March 1991 and became a constructive total loss. After being sold and renamed **Casper** in November 1992 she became the subject of a preservation attempt and was moved to Zaandam. There she remains in dilapidated condition but still with all her original fittings. It would appear that no individual or preservation group has the funds to buy and maintain her.

(Bernard McCall)

We now move on to the port of Falmouth. The bunkering of ships at Falmouth dates back well over a century but it was in the 1950s that oil replaced coal. In the mid-1980s, Falmouth Docks were bought by Peter de Savary and in 1987 he established Falmouth Oil Services which purchased two tankers for bunker work. The **Falmouth Endeavour** (754gt/72) was one of these. She was built by Kurushima Dock Co Ltd at Imabari and was completed in March 1972 as **Toshitoku Maru No. 32**. She was sold to Saudi Arabian owners in 1980 and renamed **Marwah II**. Seven years later she joined the Falmouth fleet as **Falmouth Endeavour** and was fitted to handle Yokohama fenders. On 10 November 1998, this tanker was taken out of service and laid up in the River Fal at Tolverne, eventually being sold to West African buyers in Spring of the following year.

(Bernard McCall)

Tankers discharge at Eastern Wharf where the **Assurity** (2176gt/71) was photographed on 27 May 1997, almost at the end of her career under the Red Ensign. The third of three similar vessels built for Esso by Appledore Shipbuilders Ltd, she was launched as **Esso Penzance** on 30 December 1970 and delivered in June of the following year. Although of identical dimensions, each of the three was designed for specific cargoes with the **Esso Penzance** being intended for kerosene, motor spirit and some lubricating oils. With major oil companies anxious to remove their names from ships in case of adverse publicity following spillages or some similar crisis, the ship was renamed **Petro Penzance** in 1994. The name proved to be short-lived for she entered the Everard tanker fleet and was renamed **Assurity** in late July 1995. In June 1997, she was sold to Greek buyers and was renamed **Medoil II** but was detained at Grangemouth until early October when she left for Piraeus. She arrived at Aliaga for demolition on 26 April 2008.

(Dave Hocquard)

With the growth of bunkering services at Falmouth, it was necessary to ensure that supplies were always readily available and there was a steady stream of tankers bringing fuel, usually from Milford Haven. A frequent caller was the **Agility** (1930gt/90) which passes through Carrick Roads and approaches Falmouth on 18 November 2006. Delivered in June 1990 by Richards (Shipbuilders) Ltd, of Lowestoft, she was the first of two sister vessels which were technologically advanced at the time of construction. She remained in the Everard fleet until October 2007 when she was sold to Greek owners. Handed over in Dublin, she was renamed **Aegean III**.

(John Brownhill)

Ideally situated within a deep natural harbour, Falmouth first came to prominence in the 17th century when it was an important Royal Mail packet port. It lost its pre-eminence for this role in the mid-19th century when the advent of steamships and railways led to Southampton becoming the chief packet port on the south coast of England. The location was too good to neglect and in 1860 construction work on a dock system began in Falmouth, with ship repairing commencing shortly afterwards. It is County Wharf which sees most commercial cargo being handled and it was here that the *Haslo* (MLT, 1594gt/76) was photographed on 1 April 1997 shortly after arrival from Porsgrunn with a cargo of fertiliser. The ship was built at the Stocznia Gdanska im Lenina yard in Gdansk and launched on 28 January 1976. Completed in March as *Ask*, she became *Beito* in 1982, *Haslo* in 1987, *Mariam* in 2003 and *Altrans* in May 2004.

(Bernard McCall)

County Wharf is also used for repairs afloat and the completion of other work which may have been carried out in one of the port's drydocks. The **Whitmariner** (CYP, 1363gt/79), photographed when undergoing routine work on 11 April 2001, was built at the Bordeaux shipyard of Chantiers de la Garonne for French owners as **Pierre Laffitte**. In 1990, she was sold and renamed **Pallieter**, and in the following year was lengthened by 15,8 metres and *Lloyd's Register* notes that she was converted from a products tanker to a chemical tanker. She joined the fleet of John H Whitaker (Tankers) Ltd in 1998 and is usually to be found on bunkering duties in the Solent.

(Dominic McCall)

Colour photographs of coasters at Falmouth's older quays are comparatively rare. The **Dina** (NLD, 298grt/64) is seen discharging at the Harris coal yard quay on 7 January 1972, evidently a bright sunny day. This coaster was built at the Gebr. Coops shipyard in Hoogezand. Launched on 10 March 1954, she undertook trials on 15 April prior to handing over to her owner, H Klein, of Standskanaal, as **Rini**. Later in 1954 she was sold to K D J and A Veenma, of Groningen, and was renamed **Dina**. She kept this name until sold in 1974 to owners in Deifzijl by whom she was renamed **Secunda**. The following year, she was bought for £40,000 by H R Mitchell & Sons, and was renamed **Susan Mitchell**. Like other coasters in the Mitchell fleet, she often loaded explosives at the Chapman anchorage in the Thames estuary for delivery to Drogheda. By this stage in her career her mainmast had been removed. Later sold by Caribbean owners she was not renamed. Her end came on 28 November 1985 when she capsized 15 miles north of Orchila Island whilst on passage from Kingstown to Trinidad.

(Terry Neider)

There has been a huge reduction in ship repair facilities in the UK over the last two decades. Even the drydocks at Falmouth, located at an important site in the Western Approaches, have been under occasional threat of closure. Thankfully they remain open and are generally used by ferries and ocean-going ships for which they were designed. The **Rudderman** (LIB, 4842grt/94), photographed on 17 July 2002, was the third of four newbuildings ordered by Rowbotham Tankships from the Malaysia Shipyard & Engineering company in Johore. She was launched on 22 April 1993 and completed in January 1994. By this time, Rowbotham Tankships had been taken over by P&O Tankships Ltd. All four of the new ships retained Rowbotham names but had P&O liveries. Of special note is the fact that they were the first double-hulled tankers ordered by Rowbotham and, registered in Liberia, would have been the first ones not to fly the Red Ensign.

(Krispen Atkinson)

For many years, the **Diction** (189gt/63) was a familiar sight in the Falmouth and Truro area. She was used to dredge calcified seaweed, a coral-like material, in Falmouth Bay and brought this commodity to Truro, some of it being re-exported. When not working, the ship could often be seen anchored off Prince of Wales Pier, Falmouth, where she was photographed on 16 April 2003. She was built at the Richard Dunston shipyard in Hessle as a general cargo vessel, her name indicating that she was part of the London & Rochester Trading Co Ltd fleet. She was sold and converted to a suction dredger in 1984. On 31 December 2004,

Falmouth Harbour Commissioners reluctantly withdrew her dredging licence because of pressure from English Nature. The calcified seaweed was used as an organic fertiliser and soil conditioner. It is ironic that this should have happened at a time when organically produced foods are in increasing demand. A further irony is that dredging to allow deep-draughted cruise ships to call at Falmouth seems to be acceptable. The **Diction** herself was sold for conversion to a houseboat.

(Dominic McCall)

We leave Falmouth and move two miles inland to Penryn situated at the head of a creek of the Fal. Penryn enjoyed its heyday in the 18th century when it was being used to export copper and tin from several local mines. Tin was being exported to France, Italy, Spain and as far afield as Turkey. In the 19th century there were also exports of granite. With the increase in size of ships and growing importance of Falmouth, the last part of the twentieth century saw trade dwindle and only two ships were reported in 1980. The *Selectivity* (1575grt/52) was photographed at Penryn on 7 April 1974. She had arrived the previous day from Liverpool and sailed to London on 10 April. She was built by the Grangemouth Dockyard Co Ltd and handed over to owners F T Everard in July 1952. Like many other British vessels built in the 1950s she was sold to Mediterranean operators in the 1970s, in her case being bought by Cypriot-flag operators who renamed her *Ioannis* in May 1975. Her end came almost a decade later when she grounded off the coast of West Africa on 17 January 1985. At the time she was on passage from Tema to Apapa - Lagos.

(Terry Nelder)

We see the **Timrix** (499grt/65) discharging coal at Annear's coal yard on 15 May 1972. The ship was built at the Martin Jansen shipyard in Leer as **Majo**. She was launched on 16 September 1965 and handed over to Haren-based owner Captain Alois Held on 23 November. She joined the fleet of Hull-based J R Rix & Sons Ltd in 1972. After only three years in the Rix fleet, she was bought by Sugar Maritime Ltd, placed under Union Transport management, and renamed **Union Crystal**. On 16 November 1977, while on passage from Kilroot to Poole with a cargo of road salt, she developed a list in heavy weather and subsequently sank. She had been abandoned by her crew, all of whom were rescued.

(Terry Nelder)

The **Camilla Weston** (500grt/66) has just arrived at Annear's coal yard at Penryn on 25 May 1974 and is about to discharge 559 tons of coal from Blyth. She departed for London three days later. Initially named **Crouch**, she was the second of a pair of sisterships built at the Boele's shipyard in Bolnes. They were ordered by Blue Star Line, much better known for its ocean-going cargo ships, and were intended to work as feeder ships for the larger vessels in the fleet. After working in this role for five years, she was sold to Mardorf Peach & Co Ltd and renamed **Camilla Weston**, with her attractive Blue Star funnel design being replaced by the equally distinctive Sunblest design. Her end came on 15 February 1984 when she sank off the Norfolk coast after being hit by the German coaster **Larissasee** (499grt/80). At the time she was anchored during a period of fog while on passage from Tilbury to Leith with a cargo of wheat.

(Terry Nelder)

We now head inland up the River Fal and Truro River. The Fal has long been a popular river for laying up ships. The *Arena* (530gt/60) was acquired from Swedish owners by quarry operators Aram Resources plc in 1998 and arrived at Truro on 3 July 1998 where she was repaired and modified to carry a proposed 50,000 tons of aggregates annually from Belfast and also load stone at the company's Porthoustock quarry for distribution to ports on the south coast of England. For various reasons, these plans did not come to fruition and she was eventually laid up in the River Fal. She was built at the Alfred Hagelstein shipyard in Travemünde as the general cargo ship *Norsklint* and was renamed *Carina* following sale in 1965. In 1969, she became *Underås Sandtag VI* when acquired by Swedish owners. *Lloyd's Register* notes that she was converted to a sand carrier in 1983 but the conversion would have taken place much earlier than that. The coaster is seen here in the Fal on 29 July 2002. It was reported in 2005 that she had been sold for use as a houseboat but, after lengthy refurbishment in Rotterdam, she departed for the Middle East and in 2006 was noted at Mukalla in the Gulf of Aden still named *Arena*.

(David T Dixon)

There are surprisingly few locations on the Truro River from which passing ships can be seen. Photographed as she navigated a particularly tortuous stretch between Malpas and Truro, the **Bente Dania** (DNK, 300grt/68) is nearing the end of a voyage from St Petersburg (then called Leningrad) to Truro with a cargo of timber on 28 November 1972. At that time, the unloading of timber cargoes was a much slower job than is now the case and it was not until 5 December that she departed, heading for Rotterdam. This coaster was built at the Båtservice shipyard in Mandal and was delivered in February 1968. She remained in Danish ownership until March 1977 when she was bought by owners in Casablanca and renamed **Tayssir**. The next sale saw her bought by owners in East Africa in June 1991 who gave her back her original name by simply painting over the welded letters but she was transferred to the flag of St Vincent & the Grenadines. She sank off the coast of Kenya in August 1992.

(Terry Nelder)

Husumer Schiffswerft, in the north-west of Germany, has always had a fine reputation for building attractive coasters which have often been ordered by owners in the port of Husum. The **Ute** (DEU, 1528gt/84) is a good example, having been delivered on 29 March 1984 to Reinhold Fischer, of Husum. She remained a well-proportioned ship even after she was lengthened by 12 metres in April 1994. She was photographed on a sunny and still 18 January 2004 as she approached Truro where she loaded a cargo of calcified seaweed for delivery to Lorient. Sold to Norwegian owners in late 2004, she sailed from Hull via Hamburg to Haugesund and was there renamed **Suledrott** and converted to a self discharging vessel after being fitted with a Volvo EC360 excavator.

(John Brownhill)

Truro is situated at the end of a tidal creek of the River Fal. Its connections with the tin trade date back at least to the 12th century. It was the establishment of the port of Falmouth in the mid-17th century that put an end to Truro's expansion. The port has always suffered from difficult access with only narrow and shallow navigation channels through the mud banks, especially upstream of Malpas. At Truro it is customary for ships in ballast to swing on arrival and berth ready for departure. On 1 August 2004 the **Bay Trader** (VCT, 1055gt/80) swings off Lighterage Quay as she arrives to load a cargo of scrap. The ship was built at the

J G Hitzler shipyard in Lauenburg for Union Transport as **Union Arrow**. In 1992, she was sold and renamed **Medunion** and was used on the River Rhône. Renamed **Silvia** in 1995 and **Medbay** in 1997, she returned to northern Europe following sale in 2000 when became **Bay Trader**. In June 2006, she was sold and renamed **Crea** then in March 2008, after a period laid up at IJsselmonde, near Rotterdam, she was sold to Turkish buyers who transferred her to the flag of Moldova and renamed her **Med K**.

(John Brownhill)

We now look at ships berthed at Truro. On 27 June 1972, the **Lucie Vollmers** (DEU, 498grt/56) lies at Truro with her deck cargo of timber from Kotka partly unloaded. The ship was built at the Hugo Peters shipyard in Wewelsfleth. She left northern Europe in 1973 when bought by Greek owners who gave her the name **Dionisis**. Sold on five years later, she became **Pagasitos**. Registers suggest that she was renamed **Skiathos** in 1987 but there is photographic evidence of her thus named alongside at Skiathos in June 1986. The next stage in her career was also a subject of debate for it was reported in 1995 that she had been sold to British owners for use in the Shetland fish farm industry. In fact, she remained in Greece. It was reported that she had been renamed **Ioanna-Chrysoyla** in 2003 but she carries the transliterated version of her name, **Joanna Chrisoula.** She remains at work in the Greek islands and is in superb condition.

(Terry Nelder)

In the 1950s and 1960s, small coasters sailed to the heart of the city but trade is now concentrated at Lighterage Quay, a mile downriver from the centre. The **Ilse Suhr** (DEU, 499grt/50) awaits the commencement of discharge of her timber cargo on 18 August 1972. She was built at the Bodewes shipyard in Martenshoek for well-known Amsterdam-based shipowner Spliethoff, the names of whose vessels have traditionally had the suffix -**gracht**. This coaster began life as **Brouwersgracht** and became **Beursplein** after sale in 1964 to Guus Spliethoff's Pleinlijn, based in Rotterdam; Guus was the nephew of the Amsterdam owner. This proved to be short-lived for she was acquired by a German owner in the following year and was renamed **Ilse Suhr**. A decade later, she was bought by Cypriot-flag operators and renamed **Georgios B** but was lost off Guernsey on 16 December 1975.

(the late Peter Townsend, World Ship Photo Library)

The **Cementina** (COM, 1096gt/60) has become the most frequent visitor to the port In recent years and is a remarkable survivor. She was built by A/S Longesunds Mek Verksted in Norway for Dalen Portland Cementfabrik. Launched on 15 August 1960, she was one of the first purpose-built cement carriers in northern Europe and was notable in being able to carry bulk cement in four silos and also bagged cement. In 1979 she was sold to American operators and renamed **Halliburton 602**. She was used to convey cement for use in construction work associated with North Sea oil development. Sold again in 1988, she was renamed **Curlew**, becoming **Kabedi** two years later. Having arrived at Otterham Quay on 21 October 1990, she was laid up and arrested, eventually being sold for demolition at Bruges in Spring 1991. She was, however, immediately resold for further trade, renamed **Cemking**, and became **Cementina** in 1999. On 4 December 2001, she delivered the first cargo of bulk cement to Truro. A further remarkable development is that she was lengthened by almost 12 metres at Liepaja in Spring 2003. She survived a further threat when she grounded during heavy weather off the Dutch coast in November 2006. She was photographed berthing at Lighterage Quay on 2 August 2004.

(Krispen Atkinson)

We have already commented on the Fal being a popular location for laying up ships. A combination of deep water and sheltered moorings makes it ideal. Its popularity is enhanced by comparatively reasonable fees. On 30 September 2003, the **Cementina** is seen heading downriver after discharge at Truro. On the far right. the **Mærsk Recorder** (DIS, 6292gt/00) is arriving at her lay-up moorings. Between the two ships is the **Murmansk Night** (BHS, 7395gt/90) whilst the **Issli** (MAR, 1277gt/78) is beyond. Just visible at the far left is part of the King Harry Ferry vessel that provides the only river crossing between Falmouth and Truro and thus saves a lengthy detour by road.

(T & K Atkinson)

When the **Cementina** is not available, other vessels are chartered to import cement. One such ship is the **Noblesse-C** (NLD, 1095gt/80). Like many vessels used in the cement trade, but not **Cementina**, she began life as a conventional coaster and was converted to a cement carrier later in her career. She was built at the Bodewes shipyard in Hoogezand and launched as **Noblesse** on 1 February 1980. Delivered the following month to Beck's Scheepvaartkantoor, she served this company until sold to Cebo Marine in 1998. She arrived at the Oranjewerf shipyard in Amsterdam on 24 August 1998 and was there fitted with the tanks from an earlier converted cement carrier, the **Carine** (999grt/69). Cebo Marine took delivery of her at Zeebrugge on 11 October 1998. She is seen here on 17 April 2003, it is worth noting that she berths with her port side to the quay, thus being an exception to the general rule.

(Bernard McCall)

It is appropriate that we leave the Falmouth and Truro area with this view of the **Noblesse-C** heading down the Truro River after leaving Lighterage Quay on 12 April 2006. Just coming into view by the bow of the coaster is one of the pleasure boats which provide trips from Falmouth's Prince of Wales Pier. These boats certainly offer the best views of the Fal, Carrick Roads and Truro River although it should be noted that the trips terminate at Malpas rather than Truro during periods of low water.

South of Falmouth, the Helford River flows due west into Falmouth Bay. At the limit of navigation on the river is Gweek which prospered along with the mining industry. Tin and copper were exported whilst coal and timber were imported. The final commercial trade was the import of domestic coal, although maritime interest continued when the quayside became a base for a company involved in undersea survey work. The **Greta-C** (481grt/62) was photographed at Gweek on 14 June 1973, after arrival from Goole with a cargo of coal. She sailed to Par two days later. This coaster was built at the Delfzijl yard of Niestern Sander and launched as **Westland Trader** on 20 December 1962. She was delivered as a conventional coaster with two 2-tonne derricks on 21 July 1963. Four years later she was lengthened by 8,7 metres and was converted to a container vessel. Her cargo gear was removed and her hatch coamings were raised. In 1972 she was purchased by Carisbrooke Shipping, based on the Isle of Wight, and was renamed **Greta-C**. In April 1974, she went to the yard of Drypool Engineering in Hull for conversion back to a general cargo ship but with flush deck. On 7 September 1974, she sank 14 miles off the Dorset coast when on passage from Dean Quarry to her home port of Cowes with a cargo of stone. Sadly her Master was lost.

(Terry Nelder)

As might be expected for a vessel of her age, the *Tagri* (NLD, 267grt/31), seen at Gweek on 12 July 1972 also with coal from Goole, has a fascinating history. She was built at the Rotterdam shipyard of A de Bakker and launched in April 1931. She was delivered on 6 June 1931 as *Anna* and served her Dordrecht-based owner until March 1942 when she was requisitioned by Germany. Three months later, she entered service with the Kriegsmarine at Kiel as a radio test vessel for submarines, working between Kiel, Bergen and Le Havre. She was sunk by Allied forces at Kiel in April 1945 and raised in December of that year. Returned to the Dutch government, she was repaired and rebuilt at the K A Brink shipyard in Rotterdam and again named *Anna*, entered service for the Dutch government. In March 1949, she was sold to a Dutch owner and renamed *Antares*. On 14 August 1949, she stranded north of Den Helder but later refloated. She was renamed *Tagri* when bought by T Ritskes in September 1954. She remained in his ownership until April 1976, being fitted with a new English Electric engine in 1971. In April 1976, she was sold to Panamanian-flag operators for service in the Caribbean and was fitted to carry 25 passengers. On 4 January 1981, she sprang a leak when on passage from Isla San Andres to Barranquilla, Columbia, and she foundered after her crew of eight had been rescued by a Norwegian bulk carrier.

(Terry Nelder)

South of the Helford River is the Lizard peninsula. A four-mile stretch of coast in the area is riddled with the remains of stone quarries and they have determined the character of the villages. Beaches have been formed by the longshore drift of quarry spoil. Most of the cottages were once the homes of quarrymen. A few are still lived in by their descendants but many are second homes. At the westernmost end of the peninsula are two quarry jetties of which the most northerly is Porthoustock.

The **Eileen M** (870grt/66) was one of five ships built in the 1960s for Metcalf Motor Coasters by the Burntisland Shipbuilding Co Ltd. She was launched on 19 April 1966 and completed in July of that year. In 1977 she was lengthened by 37 feet (11,27m). Sold to Caribbean operators in 1984, reports said that she would be renamed **Celt Pioneer** and then that she had been renamed **Caerleon** but there is no evidence of a change of identity. After being laid up with surveys overdue in the mid-1980s, she appears to have been returned to service and is still listed, though without owner or manager, in the 2007/08 *Lloyd's Register*. The photograph was taken on 3 December 1972. She had arrived from Cork and sailed later to London.

(Terry Nelder)

After falling into disuse, the quarry was reactivated in the early 21st century and once again sees exports of stone. Comparison of these two photographs shows many changes over the intervening years. Showing the loading facilities in the 21st century is this photograph of the **Independent** (BRB, 2113gt/82) on 9 August 2007. A ship with an interesting history, she was built at the VEB Neptun shipyard in Rostock as one of a class of six supply vessels for the navy of the former Democratic Republic of Germany (East Germany). Originally named **Mönchgut**, she was sold to Norwegian owners in 1991 and renamed **Eide Rescue V** and then **Marpol Gyda II** and **Fjellvang** in 1994. Because of their original role, the ships in the class were difficult to operate as successful conventional cargo ships and this example was lengthened by 15,4 metres in 1998. Renamed **Duobulk** and with a much increased deadweight, she was more successful commercially. It was in 2004 that she was sold again and renamed **Independent**, now managed in the UK and working usually in the aggregates trade.

(Bernard McCall)

The tiny village of Porthoustock is approached by a winding lane from St Keverne and is little more than a beach around which nestle a handful of cottages. The pebble beach has become popular with divers because there are many shipwrecks in the area around The Manacles just offshore. The beach is also an ideal location for taking photographs of ships as they load at the jetty and it was from the beach that the *Trinity* (BRB, 997gt/86) was photographed soon after arrival on 16 November 2005. Built at the Bodewes shipyard in Hoogezand as *Triton* for Beck's Scheepvaartkantoor and delivered in April 1986, she was renamed after entering the fleet of Faversham Ships and being renamed *Trinity* in mid-January 2003. In 2005, she was a frequent caller at Porthoustock.

(Bernard McCall)

Once again we see the *Trinity* but this time it is from the crewman's viewpoint on 22 October 2005. The hatch covers are being rolled back and loading is about to commence using the conveyor on the quayside. The ship delivered this cargo to Ipswich. The jetty can accommodate only one vessel at any one time and ships arrive approximately three hours before high water so that they can load and leave on the same tide. The maximum length of ship is 82 metres.

The area is a fruitful source of interest for industrial historians and archaeologists. There are the remains of industrial railways and across the bay from the quarry wharf is a large stone structure built out into the bay. Some sources suggest that this was a stone mill but rather it was a silo to which stone was brought by rail from quarries in the area. Ships were loaded from this silo. Part of this silo can be seen at the far left of the lower photograph on page 52. During World War 2, the quarry at Porthoustock produced a huge quantity of stone for airports in Cornwall and further afield.

(Dominic McCall)

Dean Quarry, south of Porthoustock, was opened towards the end of the 19th century. Although some of the stone was used at the time for local roads, much was exported. There seems to have been a lull in quarry activities between the two World Wars, but the quarry once again began to be busy when acquired by L G Thom and Co. A high vantage point allows us to look down on the

Arklow Marsh (IRL, 1524gt/88) as she loads for King's Lynn on 31 March 2003. Built at the Hugo Peters shipyard in Wewelsfleth, she was launched on 23 April 1988 and handed over Arklow Shipping on 26 May. She was sold to German owners and renamed **Fehn Trader** in 2004.

(Tony Whitty)

After purchase by L G Thom & Co, Dean Quarry was used principally for supplying the London market. This remained the main destination of the stone throughout the second half of the 20th century. It was not unknown for coasters passing in ballast to be offered a cargo to deliver to the Thames. Photographed arriving at the quarry jetty on 28 July 2000 in readiness to load a cargo for London is the *Sea Hawk* (BHS, 1602gt/77). She is one of a comparatively small number of coasters built in Japan for ownership in northern Europe. She is a product of the Kanrei Zosen K. K. shipyard in Tokushima and was launched on 4 April 1977. She was delivered to Freight Express Seacon Ltd in July 1977 and initially traded as *Sea Humber* under the flag of Singapore. This photograph is of special interest as she was about to load her first cargo as *Sea Hawk*, the name change having been made on the previous day. She reverted to *Sea Humber* at Leith on 3 July 2002 and traded under this name for almost five years. Whilst at Ipswich on 9 May 2007, she was handed over to new owners and renamed *Nildiya*. She eventually departed for Eleusis on 21 July.

(John Brownhill)

During the 1990s, coasters from the Lapthorn fleet were frequent callers to load stone at Dean Quarry. The **Hoo Maple** (794gt/89) is a typical example, photographed on one of her many calls in 1996. Built by the Yorkshire Dry Dock company in Hull, she was launched on 3 June 1989 and handed over in September of that year. In 1995, she was fitted with an excavator for self-discharge and this is being used to level off the cargo in the aft section of her hold in this photograph. She was sold out of the Lapthorn fleet in early 2004 and arrived at Newport, Gwent, on 6 April 2004. During the following year, she underwent an extensive conversion to equip her for work as a sand dredger in the Bristol Channel. Named **Argabay**, her gross tonnage was modified to 756 as a consequence of her rebuilding.

(Tony Whitty)

Operated by RMC at the start of the 21st century, the days of Dean Quarry seemed suddenly to be numbered when RMC was taken over by CEMEX, a multinational cement and aggregates company, in March 2005. Indeed it was only two months later that the announcement came saying that exports from the quarry were about to cease. The **Ladoga 16** (RUS, 1590gt/79) was loading one of the final cargoes. As we have noted already, Russian ships, especially the sea/river types, started to be frequent arrivals at all the china clay ports in the 1990s. The **Ladoga 16** was photographed on 11 June 2005. She had arrived from New Ross and was loading for London, thus able to earn some revenue on this part of her voyage back to Scandinavia. She was sold to Georgian-flag operators in 2005 and renamed **Aras 6**. She is one of nine sisterships which were all built at the Rauma-Repola shipyard in Uusikaupunki, Finland.

(John Brownhill)

Our journey westwards takes us next to Penzance which came to prominence initially as a fishing port and also for exports of tin. Between 1766 and the mid-1880s, there were a series of schemes to extend and develop the port area. The **Peroto** (488grt/79) approaches Penzance from Rotterdam on 16 January 1977. Of 361grt, this coaster was built at the Gebr Schürenstedt shipyard at Bardenfleth on the River Weser. She was delivered as **Magula** to her German owner, Gerhard Ahrens, on 11 February 1962. Following a sale in 1970, she was renamed **Bogumila** although some sources suggest that she also carried the name

Erika Anita briefly prior to that in 1970. She entered the Cornish Shipping fleet on 2 October 1974 and was renamed **Peroto**. Her name derived from the first two letters of the Christian names of the brothers who owned Cornish Shipping Ltd, Peter, Robert and Tony Goulding. Sold on in 1978, she was renamed **Rover T** and traded as such until arrival and lay-up at Rochester in July 1988. She was sold for demolition in Bruges and left Rochester in tow on 20 October 1988.

(Terry Nelder)

Built by the Rolandwerft shipyard at Berne on the River Weser, the **Island Commodore** (589grt/71) was launched on 29 January 1971 and handed over to Commodore Shipping two months later. She was lengthened in 1977. In 1990, she was sold to Huelin Shipping and renamed **Huelin Dispatch**. A further sale in 1996 saw her name shortened to **Dispatch** and this was shortened still further to **Patch** later that same year. The following year, she was detained in Viana do Castelo with many deficiencies and remained there until 2003 when she became **Nader II**. She did not appear in movement reports, however, until early 2007 when she was noted in the Mediterranean as **Captain Nader**. We see her berthed at the North Arm in the Wet Dock on 18 March 1975 after she had emerged from drydock. She had arrived at Penzance from Guernsey on 13 March and she was in port for one week, sailing to Le Havre on 20 March.

(Terry Nelder)

The **Supremity** (698grt/70) was photographed on the western side of the Wet Dock on 12 June 1980. The third vessel of this name in the fleet of F T Everard, she was built by the Nieuwe Noord Nederlandse shipyard in Groningen and was designed specifically for the liner trade between Scandinavia and Ireland. Her two 11-tonne and two 5-tonne cranes gave her a distinctive appearance. After a decade in the Everard fleet, she was sold to Cardiff-based Charles M Willie (Shipping) Ltd and renamed **Celtic Crusader**. After only three years she was sold and renamed **Korimu** by owners who transferred her to the flag of the Cayman Islands. Now flying the flag of Panama, she is still listed in *Lloyd's Register* but does not appear in movement reports.

(the late Peter Townsend, World Ship Photo Library)

When photographed on 19 July 1971, the **Pertinence** (868grt/58) had clearly just emerged from overhaul in Holman's drydock. The ship was built by Clelands (Successors) Ltd at Wallsend. In 1979 she was sold to an owner who had ambitious plans to revive maritime trade at ports in the Solway Firth. She was totally unsuitable for her intended role. Renamed **Caroline**, she was laid up at Annan and was eventually scrapped there after vandals had already inflicted their own share of damage. The church in the background is St Mary's, the construction of which began in 1832. The town's name comes from the Cornish Pen Sans, meaning "Holy Headland". Headland chapels were common in Cornwall and had several purposes. They were shrines to saints who were believed to protect travellers in addition to being navigational aids, places of refuge and lookout posts.

(the late Peter Townsend, World Ship Photo Library)

The **Nimrod** (399grt/48) had the distinction of being a traditional Dutch coaster which kept her original name despite being owned by several British owners in her later years. She was launched on 30 August 1948 at J G Bröerken's Scheepswerf "Westerbroek" yard and was completed for delivery on 7 December of that same year. She seems to have traded without incident for 22 years, being sold to a Jersey-based operator in December 1970. Having passed through the hands of two further owners, her end came on 14 November 1977 when she capsized and foundered off the Norfolk coast whilst on passage from Whitstable to Leith with a cargo of hurling stone. With crewmen seemingly in the process of painting the forestay, she is seen at Penzance on 21 August 1972 four days before departure to Ballina. She had arrived from Dunkerque on 16 August.

(Terry Nelder)

Cornish ports saw a regular stream of Romanian ships. They were certainly a frequent sight at Fowey where they loaded china clay but they also called regularly at Penzance. On 9 June 1976, the **Palas** (ROM, 1544grt/72) would almost certainly be discharging plywood that would be used in the manufacture of packing crates for broccoli. She had arrived seven days earlier from Constantza and departed for Dover on 11 June. She was built at the Santierul Naval shipyard in Constantza and was one of four similar ships built at the yard for the Romanian merchant fleet; eleven of the type had already been constructed for the Soviet fleet. The ships had three holds and three hatches which were served by two 5-tonne derricks. The **Palas** was sold in 1993 to become **Freedom Star 4** but reverted to **Palas** two years later. She has since had a succession of names, becoming **Best 2** (1997), **Nova Destiny** (2000), **Cristi** (2001), **Tara** (2002), **Jihad** (2005) and **QSM Coaster** (2006).

(Terry Nelder)

An unlikely vessel to be noted at Penzance on 16 July 1978 was the **Glenetive** (199grt/70). She had arrived the previous day with a cargo of coal from Swansea and departed for an unspecified Irish Sea port on the next day. She was built by the Malta Drydocks Corporation Ltd for Eggar, Forrester (Holdings) Ltd with management initially in the hands of Gillie and Blair. Launched on 23 March 1970, she was delivered as **Wib** just over one month later on 26 April. By 1975,

management had passed to Glenlight Shipping Ltd and she was renamed **Glenetive** the following year. In 1990, she was sold and renamed **Boston Trader** but her career was cut comparatively short when she sank some 125 miles off the coast of Mozambique on 30 July 1991 whilst on passage from Durban to Pemba.

(Terry Nelder)

A drydock had opened in 1810 but this was replaced by a newer drydock in the 1880s because the older one had been destroyed during other harbour works. A new road was built to provide access to the railway station and a swing bridge was constructed to allow access to the drydock. This historic bridge, Ross Bridge, remains in use. In recent years, the cement carrier **Ronez** (870gt/82) has been the most frequent user of the drydock facilities at Penzance and we see her here passing through Ross Bridge and entering the Abbey Basin from the Drying Harbour on 26 July 1999. Built by Scheepswerf van Goor at Monnickendam, she was launched on 19 September 1981 and delivered in February 1982.

(Tony Atkinson)

About three miles south of Penzance is the port of Newlyn, the most important fishing port in Cornwall, its pre-eminence due largely to extensive harbour works carried out between 1866 and 1888 which resulted in excellent harbour facilities being available. Until the late 1980s, there were frequent exports of stone from the port's South Pier. Seen at Newlyn on 10 September 1972, the Famagusta-registered **Agia Marina** (CYP, 2512grt/51) was about to sail for Hamburg having arrived from Nantes two days earlier. She was a product of the Weser Seebeck shipyard in Bremerhaven. She was built for German owners as **Hestia** and became **Agia Marina** in 1970 when purchased by Cypriot-flag operators. In 1973, she was renamed **Ta Hung**, later becoming **Cheng Ting** in 1976, **Tailat** in 1977 and finally **New Formula II** in 1980. That name must have been short-lived for she was demolished in Hong Kong in the same year.

(Terry Nelder)

Ships in the Comben Longstaff fleet were frequent callers at Newlyn. The **Sussexbrook** (1596grt/70) is seen at Newlyn on 29 April 1973. She had arrived earlier from Dublin and was waiting to load stone for London. She was built at Selby by Cochrane & Sons Ltd. Launched on 11 December 1969, she was delivered to Comben Longstaff in April 1970. After thirteen years in the fleet of this company, she was sold to Italian owners and renamed **Ieranto**, becoming **Ida Erre** five years later. Later sales saw her become **Sonar Prima** (1990), **Gold Star I** (1995), **El Condor** (1996), **Megane** (1997) and **Frosina** (1998). In 2005, she was bought by owners in Albania and renamed **Shkodra**. She continues to trade as such but since this sale she has been detained on several occasions as a result of port state control inspections and we must assume that she is in poor condition.

(Terry Nelder)

The **Dorsetbrook** (1328grt/57) had an interesting beginning. She had been ordered from Clelands (Successors) Ltd at Wallsend by the Williamston Shipping Co Ltd which was taken over by Gowan Shipping Co Ltd before the ship was completed. She was completed in November 1957 and Comben Longstaff & Co Ltd acted as managers. She was sold in April 1973 to Eskgarth Shipping Co Ltd and was renamed **Dorset Queen** and a sale exactly a year later saw her become **Gomba Progress**, then becoming **Altantic Progress** in 1976. Two years later, she was acquired by Cypriot-flag operators and renamed **Chrysanthi**, becoming **Lydia** in 1984 when bought by Greek owners. The photograph was taken on 13 June 1971. Arriving from Plymouth the previous day, she was loading for London. The **Fretherne** (351grt/50), built by Terneuzensche Scheepsbouw, had

arrived from Littlehampton and sailed the next day to Portsmouth. She was owned by Captain Kenneth Shaw, one of a comparatively small group of British captain/owners. After being laid up at Norwich, she was sold in June 1981 to East Anglian fertiliser manufacturer John Parsons who renamed her **Jonsue** and traded her regularly to his private wharf at Fosdyke. Taken out of service in 1986, she remained at Fosdyke as a static training vessel. Five years later, she sank at her berth and was scrapped in situ. Of particular note is the diesel-hauled train on the quayside. Stone coming from quarries at nearby Penlee Point and Castle an Dinas, about four miles north of Penzance, was brought along the Pier to the loading conveyor by this narrow-gauge railway system.

(Terry Nelder)

We leave Penzance and Newlyn in the company of the **Gry Maritha** (590gt/81) as she crosses Mount's Bay on 12 August 2005 at the start of a voyage to the Isles of Scilly. Penzance has long been an important departure point for air and sea services to the Isles of Scilly. In recent times, freight has been taken by the pallet carrier **Gry Maritha** built for Norwegian owners by Moen Slip & Mek Verksted in Kolvereid and delivered in July 1981. When sold to the Isles of Scilly Steamship Co Ltd in September 1989, she retained her original name. She is expected to be taken out of service in 2009, by which time it is hoped that the future of the sea link to Scilly will have been decided. In the background of this view is St Michael's Mount, a steep granite island topped by a castellated castle. It is connected to the mainland by a causeway at low water. It received its name following a "visitation" by St Michael in the 5th century.

(Dominic McCall)

We now travel around Land's End and move to the north coast of Cornwall where our first port of call is Hayle which typifies a port built to serve local industry. Tin was smelted here in the early 18th century and later a copper smelting works was transferred from Camborne to a site known since then as Copperhouse. In 1779, a foundry was established to manufacture pumping engines and other equipment for use in the mines. There was bitter rivalry between the owners of the copper works and the owners of the foundry, with each trying to develop their own quayside facilities and being prevented by the other. The ultimate result was that two long quays were built. The foundry closed in 1904. A railway link to the port from mines near Redruth in the 1830s meant further expansion. There was also shipbuilding at Hayle. On 17 May 1972, the **Falkur** (FRO, 299grt/65) was loading

scrap for Bilbao. Launched on 28 April 1965, the ship was built at the H C Christensen shipyard in Marstal and was one of nine similar ships. In April 1977 she was sold to H C Grube, of Marstal, and was renamed **Jenka**. As such, she traded worldwide as did many Danish coasters of her size despite their modest dimensions. In August 1983, she was sold to owners in Tahiti and renamed **Auura Nui II**. There is surprising uncertainty about the end of her life. One source says that she was demolished in March 1998 but another claims that she became a total loss on 2 September 1993. The latter seems likely because shortly after this the **Sara Boye** (DNK, 299grt/77) left Danish ownership to become **Auura Nui III**.

(Terry Nelder)

The **Yuki** (DNK, 455grt/64) had arrived from Portsmouth and was loading a cargo of scrap for northern Spain. She was launched as **Yuki Hansen** at the Slikkerveer yard of de Groot & van Vliet on 1 November 1963 and handed over to Danish owners on 13 February 1964 one week after her technical trials. In 1966, she was chartered by Ellerman Line and renamed **Iberian**. Renamed **Yuki** when sold within Denmark in 1970, she left northern Europe four years later when acquired by owners based in Beirut and renamed **Rabunion III**. She would have been converted to a livestock carrier at the time although *Lloyd's Register* notes that this conversion was made only in 1982. She met her end when, on passage from Beirut to Constanza, she grounded on the Greek island of Lesbos on 7 February 1986.

(Terry Nelder)

By the 1970s, the main trade was the import of coal for the power station, the only one in Cornwall, and exports of scrap. The 1990s saw very occasional imports of fertiliser. The **Vauban** (370grt/62), seen discharging a cargo of coal on 13 June 1971 prior to departing in ballast to Par, has impeccable Cornish connections having been built by the Brazen Island Shipyard Ltd in Polruan. Delivered in November 1962, her original owners were Lockett Wilson Line and her low air draught was needed for this company's London - Paris service. After passing through the ownership of two other British companies, she was sold to Cornish Shipping Ltd in 1971. Throughout these changes, she retained her original name. She did carry the name **La Belle Carole** for a short time in 1980 but this followed a sale that was never completed and her first official name change came in May 1991 when a further sale saw her become **Rolston**. She was eventually scrapped at New Holland in mid-1987.

(Terry Nelder)

Two fine British-owned coasters were noted at Hayle on 14 May 1972. Nearer the camera is the **Jonrix** (647grt/57) whose "acorn"-topped masts reveal that she was a Dutch-built coaster. Constructed by J Koster Hzn. at the Gideon shipyard in Groningen, she was launched on 9 April 1957 and was lengthened by 22' 6" (6,86 metres) in 1968. She sank in heavy weather off Dunkerque on 20 April 1973 when on passage from Plymouth to Antwerp. Her crew was saved. The **Colston** (586grt/55) was built at Bristol by Charles Hill & Sons Ltd. She was launched on 28 October 1954 and handed over to owners Osborn & Wallis on 6 January 1955.

She was built for the company's Bristol Channel coal trade. Sold in 1970 to W E Dowds Ltd, she traded further afield but could still be seen in the coal trade and almost certainly she would have brought coal from South Wales when noted here. In late 1987 she was sold to owners in the Windward Islands and departed for the Caribbean but was renamed only after a further sale in 1995. She then became **Stengard** and has since remained at work on inter-Caribbean trade with occasional visits to South America.

(Terry Nelder)

The **Esso Dover** (490grt/61) is seen at Hayle on 3 June 1973. Launched at the Poole yard of J Bolson & Son Ltd on 19 December 1960, this tanker joined the coastal fleet of the Esso Petroleum Company Ltd in March 1961. She distributed oil products from the company's two UK refineries at Fawley and Milford Haven until 1980 when sold and renamed **Cherrybobs**. Later in that year she was sold to the St Helena Shipping Company and was destined for a very different life.

Renamed **Bosun Bird**, she sailed to the South Atlantic where her new role would see her loading fuel at Ascension for delivery to St Helena. She was used as a floating fuel depot, storing fuel for the island's limited domestic requirements and also for bunkering the **St Helena** (3150grt/63), the island's supply vessel. Prior to her arrival, oil had been brought in drums from South Africa. In 1992, she was renamed **Alreen**.

(Terry Nelder)

The **Sand Wyvern** (531grt/59) was built by J Bolson at Poole and launched on 28 November 1958 as **Sand Grebe**, one of three similar vessels of which two were built at the Bolson yard. In July 1973, she was sold to Wyvern Maritime, of Padstow, and renamed **Sand Wyvern**. She was then put into service dredging sand off Padstow or Hayle for delivery to Plymouth with occasional voyages to Appledore or Barnstaple. These photographs were taken on 11 March 1975 four days after she had run aground on the notoriously difficult sand bar off Hayle. She was refloated two days later by the tug **Sea Challenge** and towed to Dartmouth for repairs.

(Terry Nelder)

The **Sand Wyvern** was a near sister of the **Sand Snipe** which we shall see on the next page. The most significant difference between the two was their engines. Whereas the **Sand Wyvern** had two 4-stroke 6-cylinder Lister Blackstone engines giving a total of 648bhp, the **Sand Snipe** was driven by a single 2-stroke 6-cylinder Crossley engine of 590bhp.

(Terry Nelder)

Contrasting with previous pages, there is certainly an air of dereliction along Hayle's main quayside in the view taken on 2 January 1997. It would be easy to assume that the dereliction extended to the **Sand Snipe** (537grt/61) which appeared to be undergoing demolition. Many have erroneously assumed that this was her fate. In fact, she was undergoing protracted surgery and was later towed to a slipway at Padstow where she was given a new stern section, wheelhouse and twin rudders prior to re-entering service as a sand dredger at Padstow. In her original state, she was a near-sister of the **Sand Wyvern** and was launched at the Bolson yard in Poole on 28 August 1961. Just visible astern of the **Sand Snipe** is the **Coedmor** (181grt/46). There is no space to provide a full history of this vessel. In brief, she was built by J Pollock Sons & Co Ltd at Faversham as **VIC 57** and became **Arran Monarch** in 1948. She subsequently carried cargoes of coal in the Bristol Channel and in 1964 was lengthened, re-engined from steam to diesel, converted to a sand dredger, and renamed **Coedmor**. After working out of Llanelli, she moved to Cornwall and generally discharged at Padstow or Hayle. Unlike the **Sand Snipe**, she was certainly scrapped at Hayle.

(Bernard McCall)

The story of the **Sand Snipe** takes us neatly to Padstow on the western bank of the estuary of the River Camel. Like many ports in Cornwall, it enjoyed great prosperity in the 18th century when used to export tin and copper; there were also imports of timber, coal and salt. There was a steam packet service to Hayle and Bristol and emigrant ships sailed across the Atlantic. Decline had set in by the end of the 19th century. Improvements were made after the Padstow Harbour Commissioners took over the port from the British Transport Commission in 1964. During the last two decades, trade has been infrequent. There were some imports of stone from Ireland in 1987 but only very occasional cargoes apart from those. The sandbanks, however, have ensured that the port has continued to be served by dredgers. The **Black Gem** (313grt/49) was built at the Dartmouth shipyard of Philip & Sons Ltd as the general cargo vessel **Wimborne**. She was launched on 11 April 1949 and delivered to her original owners, John Carter (Poole) Ltd, on 12 July. Sold in 1968, she was renamed **Jersey Castle**. Two years later she was bought by Sand Supplies (Western) Ltd and was this fledgling company's first venture into large-scale sand dredging after establishing itself in the Bristol Channel sand trade in the mid-1960s with the use of converted barges loading only about 70 tons. The **Jersey Castle** was converted to a sand dredger at Saul on the Gloucester - Sharpness Canal; she was renamed **Sand Gem**. She brought sand to the City docks in Bristol until sold in 1979. By 1981 she had been renamed **Black Gem** and was based at Padstow where she was demolished in 1990.

(Bernard McCall)

Access to Padstow is not easy because of many sandbanks including one known as the Doom Bar. To maintain navigable channels with an adequate depth of water for the fishing and leisure vessels using the port, the local Harbour Commissioners own and operate the **Mannin** (172gt/72), constructed at the Wivenhoe shipyard of J W Cook & Co Ltd. Built to serve Isle of Man ports and replacing an older dredger of the same name, she was acquired by the Padstow Harbour Commissioners in late summer 2001 and was not renamed but her port of registry was changed from Douglas to Padstow. She dredges in the port area and on the Doom Bar at the mouth of the River Camel and she is also hired by other port authorities in Cornwall. She was photographed as she moved cautiously out of Padstow harbour after completion of dredging on 1 April 1997. On the left are flats typical of modern shoreline development. The buoyed channel is at the far right of the photograph.

(Bernard McCall)

The **Gladonia** (657grt/63) was photographed as she loaded barley at Padstow on 23 October 1984. She had arrived from Newport the previous day and sailed for Ghent four days later. She was built by Goole Shipbuilding & Repairing Co Ltd and was launched on 22 August 1963, being delivered to J Wharton (Shipping) Ltd the following month. She was bought by owners in South Wales in March 1985 and was renamed **Integrity**, the aim being to deliver a cargo of second-hand vehicles to the Caribbean and there sell the ship. Rather surprisingly, the ship returned to Barry in January 1986 and was laid up for over a year. In January 1987, she reverted to her original name following sale to Avonmouth-based owners. Her next change of identity came in 1997 when she became **Samaret Jama**. Her end came after she foundered in heavy weather at Puerto Cabello on 31 December 1999.

(Terry Nelder)

We complete the book with a scene that sums up Cornish ships and trade. Future generations will look at ship registers and other reference books and assume that the **Carmen** and **Paquita** (both 696grt/71) are sisterships. Built consecutively by Scott & Sons at Bowling on the northern shore of the River Clyde, they had yard numbers of 440 and 441 respectively and their original owner was Hull-based Klondyke Shipping. Observation of this photograph of the two ships waiting to load at Par on 14 September 1986 when they were in the ownership of Cornish Shipping Ltd shows that they are not identical. The **Carmen**, loading for Aberdeen, was launched on 5 October 1970 and delivered as **Westondyke** in January of the following year. She became **Cladyke** in 1982, **Carmen** in 1983, **Miriam** in 1993,

Miriam I in 1998 and finally **Mohamed Mustafa** in 2002. There have been no reports of her movements for well over a decade. The **Paquita**, loading for La Pallice, was launched as **Fendyke** on 10 June 1971 and delivered in September of that same year. Her later career saw her being renamed **Clafen** (1982), **Paquita** (1983), **Vasa Sound** (1993), **Vauban** (1994), **Victoria I** (1997). In Spring 2000, she was laid up at Plymouth and then in September arrived at 'sGravendeel when again she was laid up. In January 2003, she was renamed **Mae** and was still at 'sGravendeel in September 2003, after which her name disappears from lists.

(Cedric Catt)

These two aerial views provide an excellent impression of the ports of Fowey and Par. On the left we see Fowey with ships berthed at the No. 4 and No. 8 jetties. The railway line to Lostwithiel stretches away into the distance beyond No. 8 jetty. Behind No. 3 and No 4 jetties is the location of the former railway sidings seen in the photograph on page 3.

It was not unusual to find the port of Par devoid of ships in recent years, even before its closure in December 2007. At the far left of this photograph can be seen Par Sands, a popular holiday area. In the lower right-hand corner are the circular settling tanks where the refined china clay is thickened. Other buildings on both sides of the harbour are dryers, stores (linhays) and preparation areas where various forms of clay are prepared according to the needs of different customers.

(Both photographs by Mike Grigg)